6556
4.12

NATURAL PARTNERSHIPS

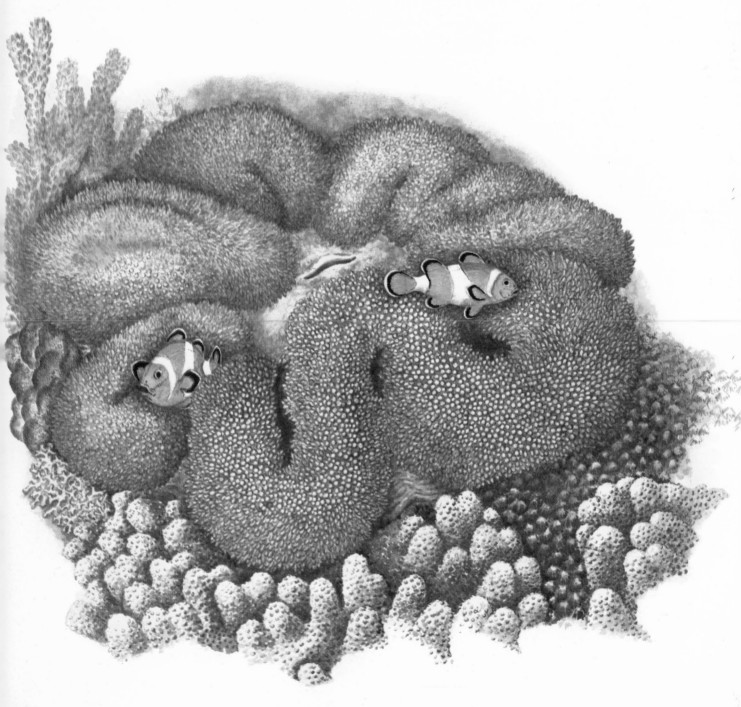

Anemone attached to coral with symbiotic fish

NATURAL PARTNERSHIPS

The Story of Symbiosis

by Dorothy Shuttlesworth

Illustrated by Su Zan Noquchi Swain

Doubleday & Company, Inc., Garden City, New York

For Linda and Tom Swain
"Together"

Acknowledgment

We are greatly indebted to the following scientists and naturalists who provided specimens and photographs and guidance in the preparation of the illustrations: Dr. James W. Atz, Mr. George G. Becker, Dr. Richard H. Foote, Dr. A. Silveira Guido, Dr. W. K. Klawe, Dr. Karl V. Krombein, Dr. Charles R. Robinson, Mr. Leonard Lee Rue III, Dr. Roman Vishniac and the Entomology Department of the American Museum of Natural History.

We are also deeply indebted to Dr. Richard D. Newsome for reading the manuscript of NATURAL PARTNERSHIPS, and giving us the benefit of his valuable criticism and advice.

Contents

Yucca plants
blooming in the desert

A Moth and a Plant

The hot sun beats down upon an already parched earth. A strong wind blows. The ground looks scarcely able to support even the scrubbiest kind of plant life. Yet, standing straight and tall in the midst of the harsh surroundings is a lovely plant with hundreds of creamy, waxlike flowers on a single stalk.

It is a yucca, which grows in the Mojáve Desert and across the grassy but treeless hillsides of southern California. A very long root extends far underground, making it possible for the yucca to take up water and providing a firm hold so that the winds do not tear the plant from the earth.

But even with water, minerals from the ground, sun, and support, the yucca still would not be able to survive if it were not for the existence of a tiny moth. The flowers would not be fertilized, for the yucca's pollen is too sticky to be carried from one flower to another by wind. And its flowers are peculiarly shaped so that they cannot be pollinated either by birds or by most insects.

Yet, as with other flowers, their grains of pollen bearing male nuclei, which develop in their stamens must reach the pistils. Hairlike tubes grow out of the pollen to reach down to the ovaries. The male nuclei are carried along and fuse with egg nuclei there—and tiny plants are started.

Because of the yucca moth, yucca plants are fertilized and can reproduce themselves. And the female moths benefit from their relationship with the yucca flowers, because the flowers provide a place in which to deposit eggs. Later the larvae that hatch from the eggs find all the food they need as they eat the seeds that are found in their "nursery."

This female moth seems to be able to choose no other plant than the yucca for her egg-laying. She gathers pollen in her mouth parts, which are shaped particularly

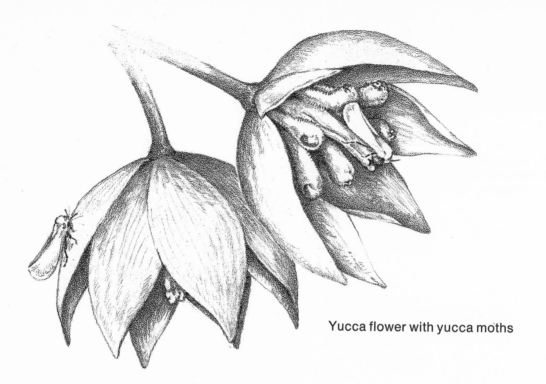

Yucca flower with yucca moths

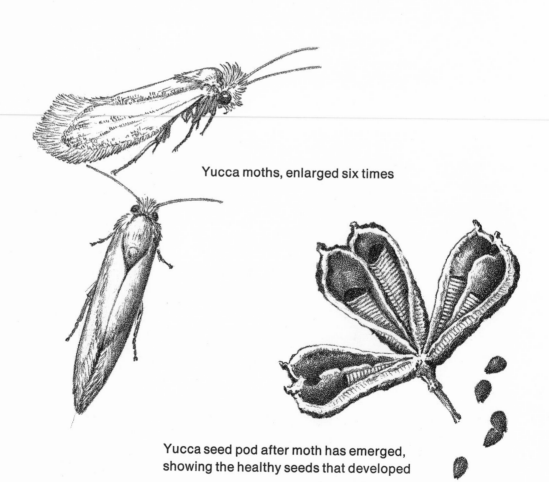

Yucca moths, enlarged six times

Yucca seed pod after moth has emerged,
showing the healthy seeds that developed

well for this activity. She then goes to a blossom on another plant and pushes down on the sticky top of a pistil (the stigma). The pollen grains are now deposited, and fertilization is possible. The yucca's black seeds can form.

With the pollen disposed of, the moth lays one or two eggs in the flower's ovary, and soon a new moth generation is on its way. Larvae hatch and feed on some of the seeds. Then larvae find their way to the ground and become pupae. The very small, pale adult moths appear and take off in an uncertain wiggle-waggle kind of flight. They are short-lived and do not have to bother about finding food for themselves because they do not eat. What they do is repeat the egg-laying process in other yucca flowers. Thus, generation after generation, the needs of insect and plant are successfully met through a working partnership

This is a famous instance of one species of living thing being closely allied with a totally different species of living thing, with both benefiting from the partnership. But it is far from being the only instance! There are many fascinating partnerships in nature to be explored.

The yucca, native to dry southwestern areas of the United States, has become a popular ornamental plant in many other parts of the country. Wherever it grows, it is dependent on tiny yucca moths for fertilization. The insects spend the winter underground as pupae. In the spring they emerge as adults and each female seeks out a plant which will become her partner. When her eggs hatch in a flower into caterpillars, which live on its seeds, the plant does not suffer. Only a few caterpillars develop within a blossom, and each eats about a dozen seeds. And two hundred seeds, more or less, are produced by a single flower.

FIRE ANTS

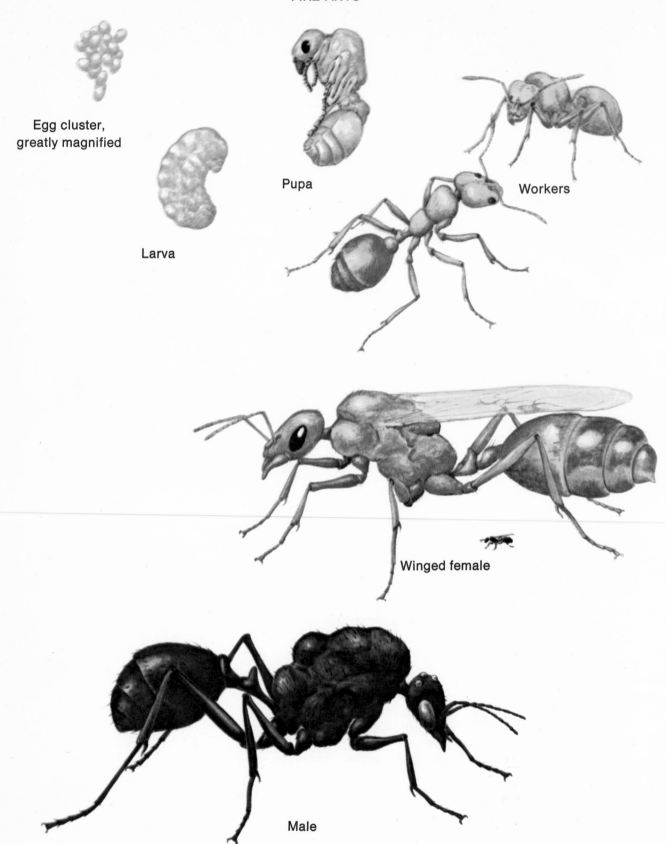

Egg cluster, greatly magnified

Larva

Pupa

Workers

Winged female

Male

The troublesome *Solenopsis saevissima richteri* ants came north to the United States from South America. In their native areas they are kept in check by another species of ant, *Labauchena daguerri*.

The Enemy Within

In some regions of the southern United States, war has been waged for a number of years against a small but mighty enemy of farmers—the fire ant. The trouble began when a few of these insects came north from South America—carried in a ship's cargo—and established themselves in their new surroundings and multiplied. Soon they became major pests. They make painful biting, stinging attacks on both people and livestock. They destroy crops. Their nest mounds of hard earth damage the blades of harvesting equipment and other machinery.

Experts from the United States Department of Agriculture fight the menace with all the weapons at their command, including chemical dusts and sprays. Though these tactics help to a degree, the fire ants continue to flourish. A very puzzling fact is that in their native South America these ants are no great problem. It might be expected that in the place of their origin, they would be even more numerous, more devastating. But this is not the case.

Finally, after much careful investigation, scientists discovered what was holding the fire ants in check in their natural habitat—other ants!

These other ants, *Labauchena daguerri*, live in the fire ants' nests. Not only do they take advantage of the shelter, they also use the food that is meant for the host ants. The effect is to weaken the colony, and the fire ants do not increase in numbers. Often a nest mound becomes so flimsy it can be washed away by rain.

Trouble begins for the fire ants when a few of the tiny invaders move into their nest, creep up on the queen and cling to her neck. They are able to hold tight without hurting her, with their jaws that are shaped and smoothed to be just right for this accomplishment. When fire ants of the worker caste approach to regurgiate food for their queen, the robber ants flutter their antennae. Somehow this influences the workers to feed them instead of the queen.

11

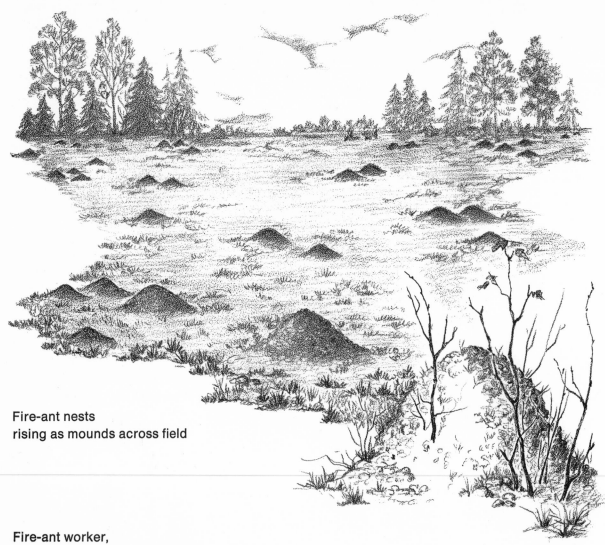

Fire-ant nests
rising as mounds across field

Fire-ant worker,
Solenopsis saevissima richteri

Okra bud
infested by
fire ants

This is just a beginning of their destructive influence. When the queen lays eggs, the invaders also lay eggs. As the larvae emerge, the fire ants give the same care to all and, carrying the double burden of their own infants and those of the invaders, work themselves to an early death. The young of *Labauchena daguerri* usually thrive. There are only males and egg-laying females—no workers among them. Soon they mate within the nest, and then fly away to enter other fire ant colonies, where again their destructive way of life is carried on.

This particular ant has never been found leading an independent life. Always it is associated with fire ants, and it seems unable to obtain nourishment in any other way than to steal the regurgitated food of the hosts into whose nest it moves. In laboratory tests *Labauchena daguerri* ants have been given suitable living conditions and provided with honey, powdered milk, and ham fat for food. But no fire ant partners were provided. Before long the little ants starved to death. It would seem that their welfare depended on having fire ants to feed them.

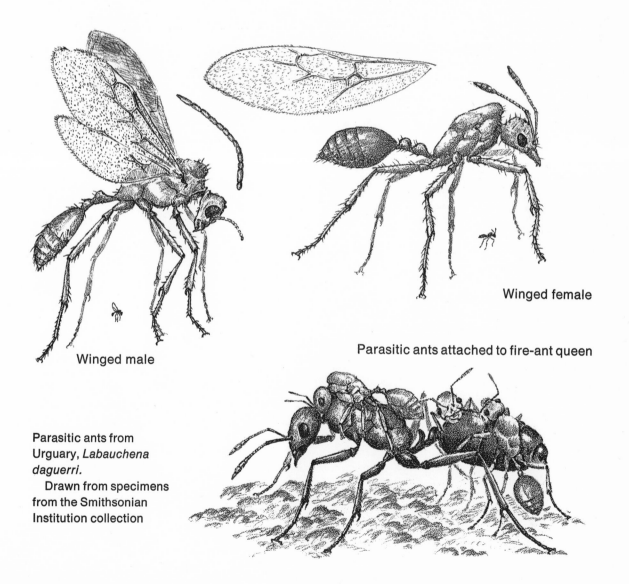

Winged female

Parasitic ants attached to fire-ant queen

Winged male

Parasitic ants from Urguary, *Labauchena daguerri.*

Drawn from specimens from the Smithsonian Institution collection

13

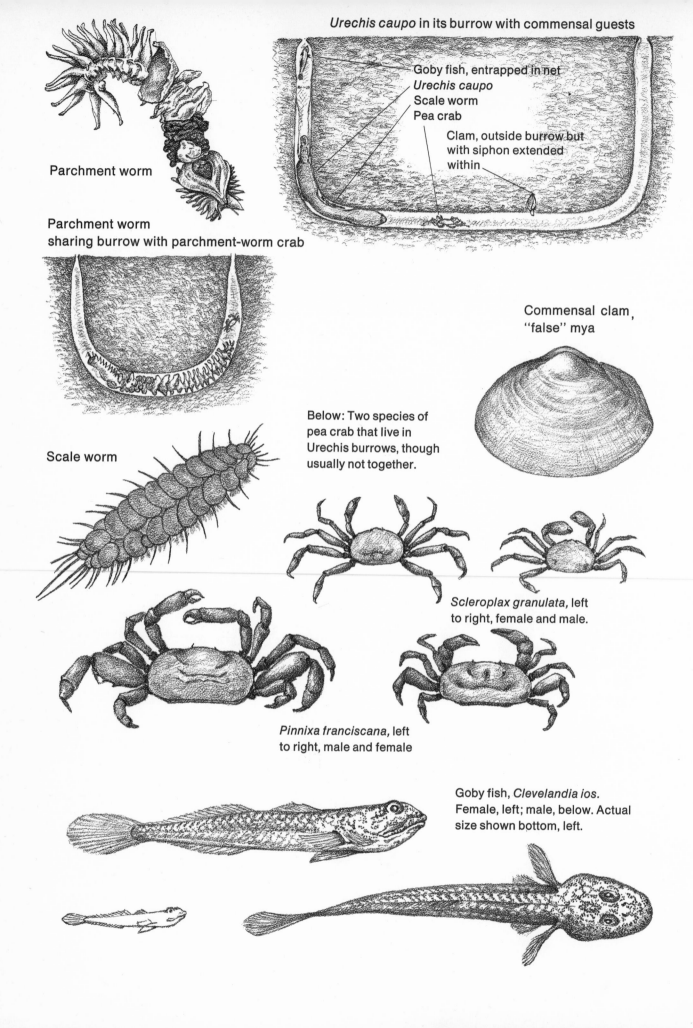

Parchment worm

Parchment worm
sharing burrow with parchment-worm crab

Urechis caupo in its burrow with commensal guests

Goby fish, entrapped in net
Urechis caupo
Scale worm
Pea crab

Clam, outside burrow but
with siphon extended
within

Commensal clam,
"false" mya

Scale worm

Below: Two species of
pea crab that live in
Urechis burrows, though
usually not together.

Scleroplax granulata, left
to right, female and male.

Pinnixa franciscana, left
to right, male and female

Goby fish, *Clevelandia ios.*
Female, left; male, below. Actual
size shown bottom, left.

The "Innkeeper"

A nature explorer poking into a mud flat along the California coast is likely to find an unusual, U-shaped burrow. Not that the burrow itself would be especially peculiar, but it would prove to be the home of an odd assortment of animals. The original owner is a wormlike creature having the scientific name *Urechis caupo*; it is this one that made the burrow. But there are other occupants—perhaps one or two small fish, one or two tiny crabs, and a worm.

The second part of the name of the burrow's owner—*caupo*—means "innkeeper" in Latin, and this is fitting for an animal that seems to act as a hotel keeper for others. At this "inn," however, there are no bills to be paid; the creatures that make use of it contribute nothing to *Urechis*. But neither do they seem to interfere with its activities or harm it in any way. If danger threatens, the crabs and worm huddle close to the "innkeeper."

Urechis belongs to a group of marine animals that early in life appear to be segmented worms, or annelids. (The common earthworm belongs to this group.) However, as they grow, the segments of the body disappear. The "worms" (they belong to the group called *Echiuroidea*) give up their free-swimming existence to settle down in various tidal zones in mud or in the cavity of a shell or coral rock.

15

The burrow that each one makes supports a small tube of mucus which *Urechis* produces, cementing one end of the tube close to the burrow's opening. After this has been done, the movement of the animal's body in the burrow causes water to be drawn through the mucus, straining out microscopic bits of food. When the tube is filled, *Urechis* swallows it, then moves up to the burrow's opening and attaches the rim of a new tube. The uninvited occupants of the burrow benefit by eating some of these food scraps, the burrow affords them a shelter, and, in turn, their activities help to draw water into the muddy, U-shaped tunnel.

The yucca moth and the plant that it pollinates, the fire ant and the ant that destroys it, *Urechis* and the creatures that live in its burrow—how varied these all are! Nevertheless they have something in common: All are part of the fascinating nature story of *symbiosis*.

Symbiosis

The word symbiosis (made up of two Greek words meaning "life together") describes a number activities found in plant partnerships, animal partnerships, and some partnerships between plants and animals. In some of these associations the activity is beneficial to both partners, as with the yucca moth and plant. Such a type of symbiosis, since mutual aid is given, is known as *mutualism*.

If one partner benefits from the association while the other suffers, it is called *parasitism*, the partner that gains being the parasite. The organism from which the parasite takes nourishment or protection is known as the "host."

When an animal or plant host feeds or shelters others without being helped or injured by them, as with the *Urechis*, the relationship is *commensalism*.

Many times people refer to the parasites, or to any plant or animal that is harmful to themselves as "bad." The helpful ones are called "good." But it should be understood that such approval of an animal, or disapproval, is purely from the human point of view. Every animal—except man—and plant lives according to the way it has evolved, and has no concern with helping or harming any other living thing.

At first it may seem that such strange partnerships have little to do with people—that they are merely natural oddities. However, while this may be true in some cases, many natural partnerships have a direct bearing on the health and welfare of humans. It would be difficult to think of a connection more intimate than that between a person and the bacteria that live within his body. The bacteria usually are parasites. They take nourishment and warmth from their hosts. Some of these bacteria are harmful; they are the "germs" that produce such dread diseases as tuberculosis, diphtheria, and staphylococcus infection.

But there are other kinds of bacteria living within the human body that are believed to be helpful partners. They do not seem to be harmful, and some of them may make it possible for the body to absorb needed vitamins from food.

The sphinx moth, a night-flying insect, is attracted to honey-suckle flowers which, after dark, have an especially strong scent. Its long proboscis draws out nectar which nourishes the moth, and at the same time the flower is pollinated.

A microbiologist at a large medical school has suggested that one of the problems for astronauts of the future is that, as they live for long periods in outer space, sterile air (having no bacteria), food, and water might drastically reduce the amount of bacteria in their systems. As a result, upon return to earth, they could suffer serious illness. It has been suggested that they be given bacteria pills to take with them.

Larger organisms can be parasites in humans too. There are roundworms which, in their adult stage, can thrive in a person's intestines—meanwhile impairing his health. Also, when their eggs are taken into the body, they may hatch into tiny larvae which enter the blood stream and cause trouble in various areas before coming to rest in the intestines.

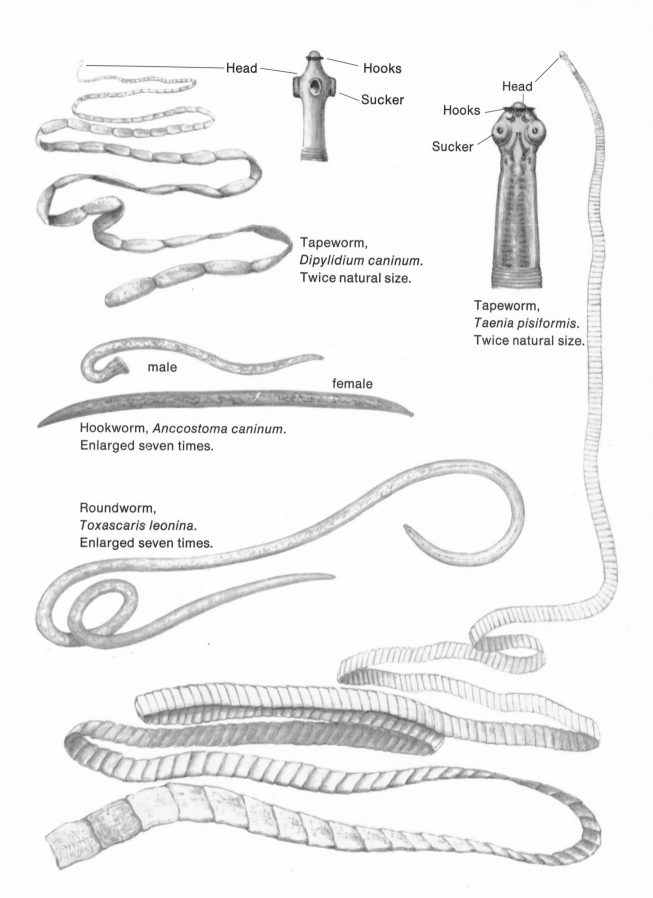

Head — Hooks

Sucker

Tapeworm,
Dipylidium caninum.
Twice natural size.

Head

Hooks

Sucker

Tapeworm,
Taenia pisiformis.
Twice natural size.

male

female

Hookworm, *Anccostoma caninum.*
Enlarged seven times.

Roundworm,
Toxascaris leonina.
Enlarged seven times.

19

Roundworms are also common pests of dogs. They can be passed on from the mother to her puppies. They can be picked up from any place soiled by another dog that has worms.

Tapeworms are still other parasites that nourish themselves at the expense of humans and animals. A dog that has become host to tapeworms is likely to eat enormous quantities of food, yet be painfully thin and have a dull, lifeless coat.

Hookworm and the "pork worm," or trichina, are two more of the all-too-well-known parasitic worms. People can avoid having the hookworms as destructive "partners" by strict cleanliness. And the trichina worms are controlled by thoroughly cooking pork before eating it.

Some kinds of worms are found only in tropical and subtropical countries. Others are more widespread. Once they are established inside a host, worms can be very difficult to dislodge. But there are medicines made of herbs and plant roots that can usually do away with them.

Not all worm parasites can pass through their various stages of development in one host. There are some, known as flukes, that require several. The liver fluke, common in the Far East, has a snail as its first partner. First, either the snail swal-

LIFE CYCLE OF LIVER FLUKE

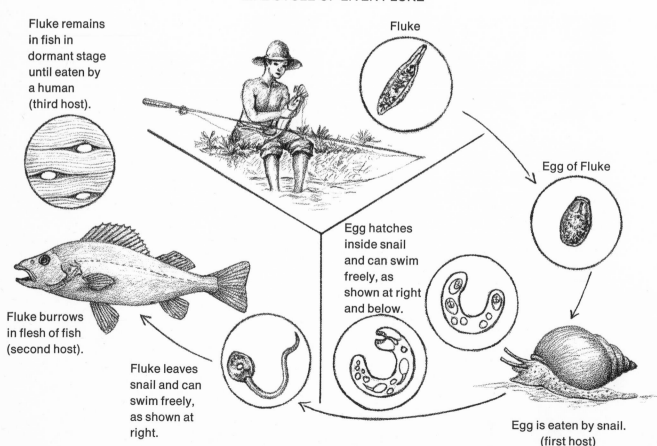

Fluke remains in fish in dormant stage until eaten by a human (third host).

Fluke

Egg of Fluke

Egg hatches inside snail and can swim freely, as shown at right and below.

Fluke burrows in flesh of fish (second host).

Fluke leaves snail and can swim freely, as shown at right.

Egg is eaten by snail. (first host)

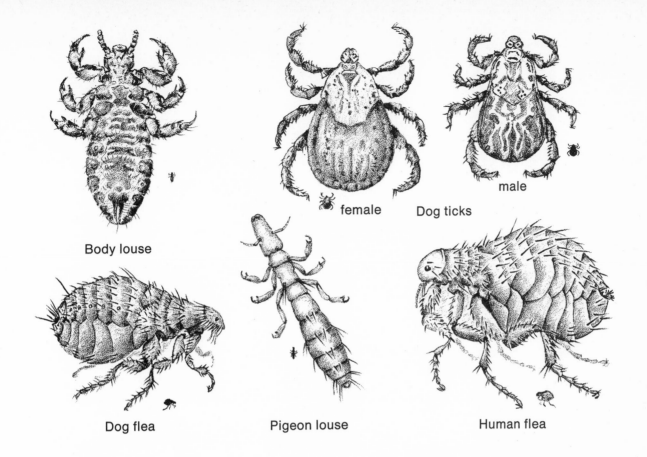

Body louse

female   Dog ticks   male

Dog flea   Pigeon louse   Human flea

lows a tiny fluke egg, or the snail is invaded by fluke larvae. If an egg is swallowed, it hatches within the snail and develops through several larval stages there, multiplying itself many times. The active larvae escape from their snail host and swim freely in the water until they encounter a fish of a certain species, which is destined to be host number two.

The flukes quickly penetrate into the flesh of this second host and there remain unless some unfortunate human eats the fish without thoroughly cooking it. At this stage the young flukes make their way to various places, perhaps the small bile passages, in the human body, attach themselves there by small but strong suckers, then feed on blood. There are several different species of liver fluke, and each has its own particular kind of snail as its partner.

Some partnerships are formed by part-time parasites which take nourishment from a host and then leave him. Ticks, fleas, and lice are well-known examples of such external parasites. And the partnerships may be so close that the parasites always go to the same kind of host. In fact, this has been noted so definitely with lice, that scientists sometimes trace relationships between various animal species through the lice they find on them.

So it is evident that some types of symbiosis do have an important bearing on people's lives and welfare. But parasites are only a small part of a very big and fascinating story. Let us look next at a remarkable partnership in the plant world.

An underwater cleaning service

Some kinds of marine creatures join forces in a useful partnership, as one cleans the other and, in doing so, obtains food. There are a variety of "cleaner fish," living both in clear tropical waters and in cooler seas. They are most numerous in the tropics, and the tropical species generally are more brightly colored. Their behavior is notable, too.

They actually do "stunts" that attract other fish which then become the willing recipients of their services as parasites and dead tissue are removed from their skin. But many fish apparently depend on this grooming and seek it voluntarily, without any "advertising" on the part of the cleaners. At least twenty-six species of fish are known to be cleaners, as well as several species of shrimp and one kind of crab. In Mexico a certain angle-fish is called *El Barbero, "the barber,"* because of the way it grooms other fish.

British soldier lichen, *Cladonia cristatella*

When Two Plants Make One

Have you ever noticed a certain kind of plant growing on a bare rock? It may have flat, gray-green foliage which lies on the hard rock surface like a doily on a table. It seems strange that no soil is involved. From what does it take its nourishment? How did it get a start on this barren spot?

A plant looking like that and living in such conditions would be a rock lichen, its existence made possible by a partnership of two plants—an alga and a fungus. To understand how the partnership works, it is helpful to examine each of the plants involved.

Algae are the simplest of green plants. Some are no larger than a single cell, such as the plants that form common "pond scum." Others are grouped together in thin sheets of cells, forming seaweed. However, none have true roots, stems, leaves, flowers, or seeds. Algae live in water or in very damp places where they are surrounded by raw materials for food-making. The cells, each of which contains chlorophyll, take in these materials through their walls and convert them into food as part of the process called photosynthesis.

Like algae, a fungus plant has no true roots, stems, leaves, flowers, fruits, or seeds. It also does not have chlorophyll. As a result it cannot make its own food, such as fats and proteins, but must take it, ready made, from other things which may be living or dead. In some fungi food-getting equipment is a white threadlike net that penetrates into the matter on which it is growing, such as bread, or that extends over the matter, such as rock. The net serves also as an anchor, for it produces a weak acid, softening the rock and making it possible for the threads to work into the surface and become firmly fastened.

In this network can be found certain algae spores—the tiny dustlike cells that serve in place of seeds. They soon grow new algae plants that take moisture and carbon dioxide from the air; and since they have chlorophyll, they *can* manufacture food—enough for themselves and their partners. Thus the rock lichen is created.

In times of drought lichens become brittle but do not die. When moisture returns, they absorb it and start growing again. However, their growth is slow. It may take many years to increase the area coverage of a lichen by as much as a few square feet.

Lichens can reproduce themselves when the fungus partner develops webs of cells in which a few algae cells are present. Sooner or later these are carried away by wind, or they fall from the parent body. If they land in a favorable spot, a new "colony" begins to grow.

The partnership of algae and fungi is not limited to gray-green rock lichens. There are thousands of species of this combination plant. Among the more colorful are the cladonias, found in gay profusion over many mountain regions in New England, on otherwise barren stretches of earth and on rocky ledges. Their growth is extremely dense and coral-like in form. One species, called the scarlet-crested cladonia, or British soldier, bears bright red reproductive organs at the top of twisted gray stalks. It thrives on old stumps and rotting logs.

Also coral-like is the bushy reindeer moss which carpets many open, sunlit areas of forests. In spite of its popular name it is not really moss; it is a lichen, a particularly hardy kind that thrives on frigid mountain tops and in arctic regions where almost no other plant will survive. It furnishes valuable food for reindeer, caribou, lemmings, and other animals that live in extremely cold climates.

A picturesque lichen is commonly known as old man's beard, for it hangs in large clusters from twigs and branches of evergreen trees of damp forests, giving them an aspect of great age. At first glance it might appear to be Florida moss, but they are not related. Florida moss is a flowering plant of the pineapple family, and it grows in southern climes.

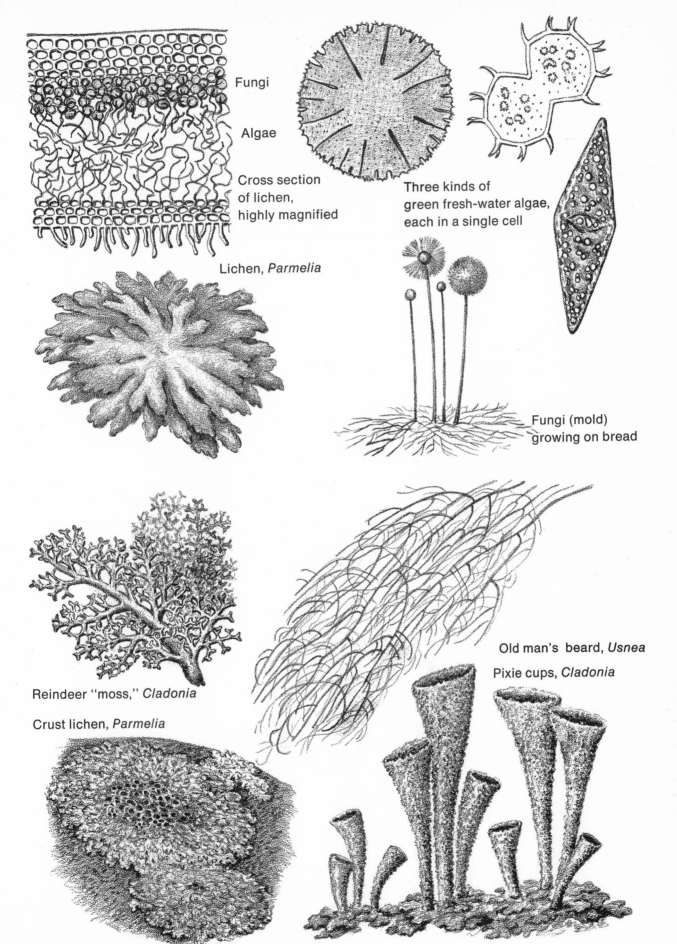

Fungi

Algae

Cross section
of lichen,
highly magnified

Three kinds of
green fresh-water algae,
each in a single cell

Lichen, *Parmelia*

Fungi (mold)
growing on bread

Reindeer "moss," *Cladonia*

Crust lichen, *Parmelia*

Old man's beard, *Usnea*

Pixie cups, *Cladonia*

25

The yellow wall lichen belongs to a group whose members, for the most part, are gray-green. But although its growth pattern is the same as the typical rock lichen, it has a bright orange color. Off the Maine coast are islands so covered with these lichens that, seen from a distance, the whole landscape has a golden-yellow hue.

Because of the acid in their make-up, most lichens are bitter to the taste. However, there are exceptions. In northern Africa and western Asia is a kind that is attached only loosely to rocks and soil, its acid being too weak to penetrate very deeply. Winds easily dislodge small pieces which roll along until they collect in some depression in the ground. Desert tribes grind such lichen into meal from which to make bread. In ancient times it was the "manna" of the Israelites.

Not all fungi form partnerships with algae. Many are parasites—taking their food from other plants and causing diseases in their host or killing it outright. Then there are others which are not partners with other plants in the close way they are with algae so that lichens are produced, but still are beneficial to their host.

In the fascinating orchid family there are certain species that have a rather unusual relationship with fungi. It is unusual because the orchids are green plants and therefore should be capable of an independent life. Nevertheless, without the

Orchid from Africa used by growers in propagation. *Ansellia africana.*

Indian pipes, *Monotropa uniflora*

presence of a certain type of fungi in the soil, these orchids simply do not thrive. The fungi are important from the time the orchid seeds are planted. They are microscopic, and are difficult to germinate in greenhouses. It is common practice for an orchid grower to place seeds in sterilized jars and coat them with spores of a fungus. Or he adds some of this fungus to the soil. Only then does he feel sure of success in producing truly beautiful flowers. Scientists do not know why this works—but it does.

The eye-catching Indian pipes, found in many woodlands of the United States, depend on partners. They are called saprophytes. An Indian pipe is white, tan, or pink, and as a result is often mistakenly called a fungus. However it is a seed plant. Each fleshy-white or pink-tinged stem bears a flower which bends downward until it has been fertilized. Then it becomes erect.

Some Indian pipes are parasitic, taking their nourishment from the roots of other plants. But for the most part they have fungus partners on their own roots from which they derive mineral and organic food.

27

Two-toed sloth, which may be host to algae or moths

Plant and Animal Partners

The algae do not limit their partnerships to joining with other plants. In some cases they form a close association with an animal.

Certain flatworms, as adults, depend on algae for their nourishment—not because they eat the tiny plants, but because they have the algae living in their tissues. When such a worm *(Convoluta roscoffensis)* is young, it is white and feeds on small organisms. But presently the little green cells begin to enter its body, and a mutual benefit begins as the algae use nitrogen wastes from the animal's body and the worm digests the green cells. It does not have to search for other food. The body of the worm takes on a rich green tone. Eventually the worm stops eating. Later the partnership is doomed as the worm uses up the last of its algae food supply. But this does not happen before the worm has laid eggs.

The convoluta worms are to be found on certain sandy beaches of France. They occur in great numbers, with thousands or even millions concentrated in an area, always where rivulets of draining water will keep them moist during low-tide periods. As the mass of tiny worms (each is a mere tenth of an inch long) lie glistening in the sun, they look like splashes of dark green paint on the sand. When the first waves of the rising tide begin to roll in, each worm instantly burrows into the sand, and the green patch disappears as if by magic. Twice in every twenty-four hours the worms rise to the surface, thus providing exposure to light for their green commensal partners; twice they dig out of harm's way, in rhythm with the tides.

Another animal that has a partnership with algae is the huge "bear's paw" clam, *Tridacna*. This greatest of all clams lives among the corals of the South Pacific, resting among the reefs with the hinge that connects its two shells on the down side. Usually the mighty clam, which may weigh as much as five hundred pounds, makes its home in shallow water. From beneath the fluted upper edges of its shells protrudes a thick purple mantle. This catches the sunlight which enables the growth of green algae within the mantle. The microscopic plants furnish a large proportion of the clam's nourishment. As it grows older, the animal uses its digestive tract less and less, seemingly depending completely on its "home-grown" plant partners for sustenance.

One of the oddest of the plant-animal combinations is that of the giant sloth and algae. The mammal—unusual enough in itself as it leads an upside-down existence in the tropical forests of South and Central America—is even more unique because of its partnership with a type of alga, which lives in the animal's coarse hair. Because of this the sloth has a greenish coloring that blends with the foliage during the rainy season when trees are most verdant. When the vegetation is dry, the algae turn brownish, and so do the sloths. As a result, the animals are afforded the protection of camouflage throughout the year as they blend into their background. Without algae, their hair is yellowish. The algae apparently do not derive any particular benefit from the sloth partner except that they are provided with a place to live.

A whole book could be devoted to the insects that use certain plants as partners for the raising of their young, because so many of them (as with the yucca moth) do this. However, with the yucca, the plant is as dependent on the moth as the moth is dependent on it. In most cases the insect is a parasite—not benefiting the plant of its choice and, indeed, often injuring it.

A commonly known insect-plant partnership is that of the milkweed butterfly and the milkweed plant. These handsome orange-and-black winged insects spend

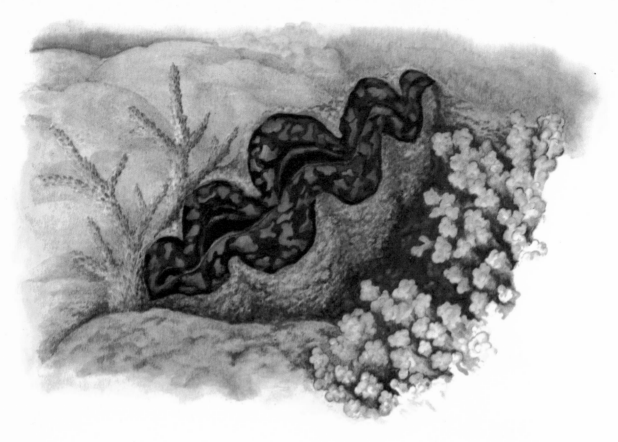

Giant clam, *Tridacna,* with protruding mantle in which algae grow

the winter months in southern regions. When warm weather is felt, they begin a northward migration, and as they travel, they lay eggs on young milkweed plants. The caterpillars which develop from them find all the food they need on the "nursery" plant, and they tear off pieces of the leaves and chew them, much as a person eats lettuce. When they develop into winged adults, however, they fly to new territories, and the plant recovers.

Other plants are not so fortunate with their unbidden guests. The potato beetle and the cucumber beetle become permanent parasites on the plants for which they are named, and do them great harm. Farmers look on them as enemies.

But there are turn-about instances where farmers deliberately use insects to destroy unwanted plants. Australia is grateful to a little moth for ridding the country of a cactus plague. In 1839 a single prickly pear cactus was taken there and presented to one of the settlers in the northeastern farmlands. Admiring it, he gave cuttings to a number of friends who planted them around their cabins—and in less than a hundred years the cacti had overrun sixty million acres of pasture land.

Some methods of killing plants, such as burning, did not prove practical for destroying them, so a study was begun of cactus-eating insects. There were a number to choose from, and each was checked for what damage it might do, besides being helpful in one way, if introduced into a foreign land. Finally a choice was made, and several thousand cactus-moth eggs were shipped from Argentina to Australia where they were placed on the spiny cactus leaves.

The eggs hatched, the larvae burrowed into the plants, and the partnership was carried to its conclusion—fatal to the cacti. Within a few years, moths were laying eggs by the million and as the larvae developing from them destroyed the plants, Australia was relieved of its problem. Happily these moths were obligate parasites on cacti, and as the cacti died away, their numbers decreased. They did not turn to any other vegetation.

A partnership in which a plant and insect are of mutual benefit—with benefit being reaped also by people—is that involving a small wasp and a fig plant. Some years ago the best-quality cultivated figs were grown only in Smyrna, Turkey. Efforts were made in California to produce equally fine fruit, but season after season there was no improvement. The figs were still not juicy. At last studies

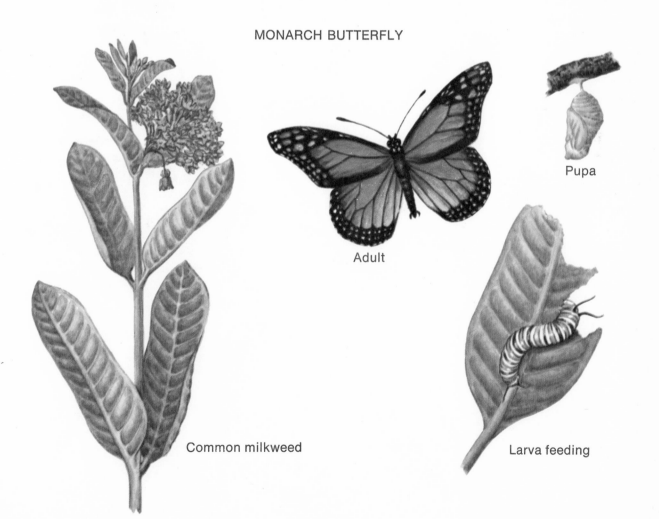

MONARCH BUTTERFLY

Pupa

Adult

Common milkweed

Larva feeding

revealed that in their native country a wasp played an important part in the figs' development. This kind of wasp forms its colony in a wild fig, the flowers of which have the short ovaries that are suited to the insect's needs. The Smyrna fig flowers have long ovaries. However, in their explorations before starting to lay eggs, the female wasps often enter the Smyrna fig flowers, fertilizing them with pollen from the wild fig. The resulting fruit grows large and tasty.

American fruit growers brought some of the wasps and some of the wild fig trees from Turkey to the United States. They placed the fruit, with colonies of wasps ready to emerge, in wire baskets, and hung them in the orchards of Smyrna fig trees when the flowers were ready for pollination. The results were successful. Now they had tasty figs.

In England there is an intriguing three-way partnership involving a blue butter-fly, a plant, and ants. Without fail the butterfly chooses a fragrant thyme bush on which to lay her eggs. Later the larvae hatch and begin to eat the purplish flowers—until ants come and carry the larvae away. The ants give the larvae shelter in their

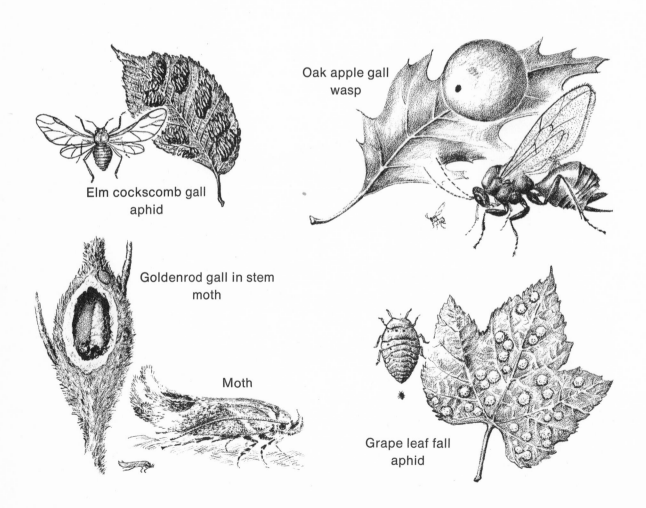

Elm cockscomb gall
aphid

Oak apple gall
wasp

Goldenrod gall in stem
moth

Moth

Grape leaf fall
aphid

nests because they can take from them secretions which they turn into honey. The larvae are not harmed, however, and when they emerge as adult butterflies, they fly off and begin their cycle of life once again by depositing eggs on thyme plants.

There is a combination of plant and insect that produces an interesting structure known as a gall. It is started when the insect inserts its egg into the stem, leaf, flower, or root of a plant. Later, as a larva hatches from the egg, it secretes a substance that irritates the surrounding tissues. As a result the tissues do not develop in a normal way, and a small bump—or gall—appears on the plant.

Gall-producing insects are varied, but all belong to one of two groups: the tiny flies, called gall midges, and the gall wasps. Some of them are a menace to food crops as they invade such plants as wheat, rye, and barley. Others do no serious damage.

One of the most picturesque of the galls is the "oak apple," created by a small fly. As this insect nibbles the leaf of its oak-tree partner and gives out the substance that affects its surroundings, threadlike fibers begin to grow out around the little

Fig wasp and fig branch with fruit

Fig wasp,
Blastophaga paenes,
greatly magnified

creature. They continue growing until they are enormous compared with the larva, and a thin, smooth covering forms around the outside of them. This makes an elaborate but snug home for the insect, which presently stops eating and changes from larva to pupa. An adult emerges as the pupal stage is completed, which at once cuts a hole in the shell-like wall of its home. Then it ends its partnership with the oak tree by flying into the great outdoors. However, when ready to lay eggs, it seeks either the tree that was its nursery or another oak to harbor its own family.

Close relationships between insects and plants seem almost endless in their variety. On the whole the partnerships may be considered a give-and-take arrangement, for at least half of all species of plants depend on insects for the cross-pollination that makes their survival possible. Looking back to the distant past in the evolution of plant and animal life, we find that as winged insects developed, vegetation flourished with ever-increasing luxuriance. Flowers became more and more showy and attractive to the insects, and they proved a source of food for

Colorful partners: insects and flowers

34

them, with their pollen and nectar. The bright colors and recognizable patterns that evolved in the flowers were the means of attracting the partners they needed for survival. Especially with bees is the connection between insect and flowers evident: The bees have become adapted in varied ways to collect nectar and pollen, while certain flowers are especially suited to attract and to serve bees.

Sometimes people have been mistaken about plant-animal partnerships when two forms of life appeared completely dependent on each other while actually they were not. One such case involves certain acacia trees of the tropics which bear hollow thorns. Ants use these to a great extent for nests, and they harvest bits of oil from the tips of the trees leaflets. The ants are ferocious; they drive away most other creatures that might seek food or shelter at their tree. As a result, the belief became popular that the acacia and ants actually needed each other for survival. However, close study has revealed that the acacias can live perfectly well without the ant tenants, and the ants can flourish in other settings.

Tropical acacia with inflated thorns
which certain ants hollow out
and use for rearing their young

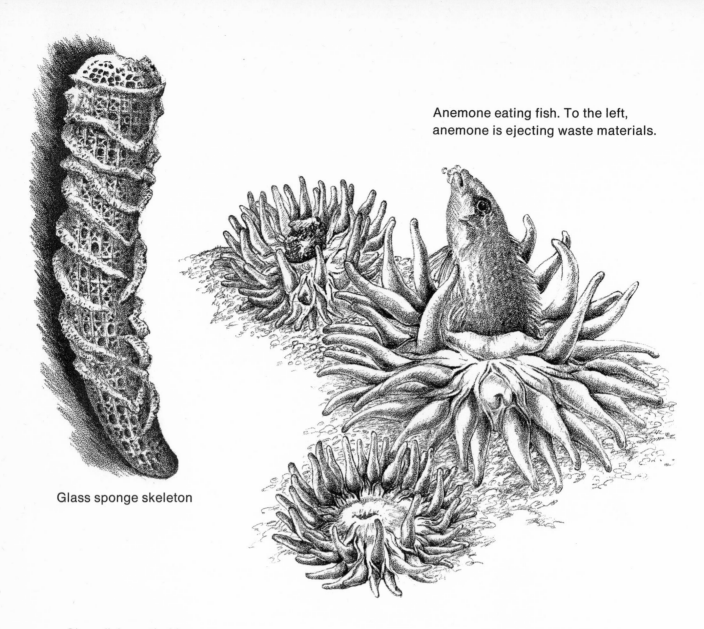

Anemone eating fish. To the left, anemone is ejecting waste materials.

Glass sponge skeleton

Clownfish nestled in tentacles of anemone

Clownfish in typical swimming pose

Underwater Partners

In Japan a sentimental wedding gift may be the skeleton of a dried-out sponge which encloses a dried pair of shrimp. This odd souvenir of the deep sea is called by a name that means "together unto old age and into the same grave."

The joining together of these two forms of animal life begins when the shrimp are small, free-swimming larvae. They enter the "glass" sponge, a kind which flourishes in the deep waters off Japan, the Philippines, and the West Indies. It takes a cylindrical form. The shrimp larvae can easily get into one of the cylinders, and there they feed on food organisms that are flowing through the sponge. After a while they reach such a size that they cannot get out of the sponge, even if they try. They and the sponge, therefore, remain together "unto old age" and death.

Another relationship between shrimps and sponges is less final. The mantis shrimp, which resembles a lobster in form and may be a foot or more in length, often lies in wait in the opening in a big, soft type of sponge. When an unsuspecting fish comes close to the sponge, the mouth of the mantis shrimp opens suddenly and, with jackknife-like action, slashes its victim.

A fascinating example of togetherness is that which exists between the colorful clownfish and the giant sea anemone of the South Seas. The anemone looks like a gorgeous underwater plant rather than an animal with poisonous tentacles. But an animal it is—and one that eats other animals. When small fish come near, they are quickly killed by the thousands of sting cells in the tentacles. Then they are carried to the anemone's mouth to be eaten.

In spite of this deadly threat to fish by the anemone, the little clownfish live in and around it in complete safety; the sting-bearing tentacles curl away from them. Even when a clownfish brushes against a tentacle, it is not stung. The anemone really is its home in the sense that clownfish get protection from danger there (their bright orange, white, and black coloring makes them easily seen by enemies), and apparently they spend their nights sheltered by the tentacles.

37

Even the nests of clownfish are made in relation to the anemone; usually they are located very close to the large partner. After eggs have been laid and hatched, the larvae spend about two weeks at the water's surface. Then, as they start to take on the color pattern of the adult, they drop to the bottom of the sea and team up with an anemone of their own. Several fish may have the same anemone as a partner.

The anemone derives some benefit from its partners. When a clownfish comes on a piece of food too large to be handled alone, it carries it back to the anemone

A detail of the man-o-war's tentacles

Portuguese man-o-war, *Physalia pelagis,* shown with a fish victim (yellow in color) entangled in its tentacles, and with its symbiotic partner, *Nomeus albula.* This kind of fish is unharmed by the sting cells on the tentacles.

and the extra morsels are passed on to the large partner. It has also been reported, apparently with accuracy, that these fish will care for an anemone that becomes unhealthy because of the condition of the sea water. They fan it, rub its tentacles, and clean it by circulating water around it.

Clownfish—also called damselfish—can exist without an anemone partner. They are successfully kept in countless home aquariums. However, this captivity affords them safety from natural enemies. It is when living among the dangers of the sea that they need all the help they can get in escaping from hungry enemies.

There are a number of other underwater animals that snare their prey with sting cells, and there are other instances where fish are strangely unaffected by the poison. Various jellyfish, including the dreaded Portuguese man-of-war, have powerful stings which can deal sudden death to almost any small fish. But the man-of-war fish, found in tropical seas, is immune to the poison and, in fact, lives within the area of the long, spreading tentacles of the creature for which it is named.

Tide pools and the rocky bottoms of seashores the world over harbor a bewildering variety of anemones. Many burrow in the sand or mud or attach themselves to seaweed, rocks or wood, such as wharf piles. But a number of them lead a roving life, attaching themselves to another animal such as a snail or crab.

Probably the most famous of such partnerships is between a hermit crab of European waters and a sea anemone, *Adamsia palliata*. A young hermit crab finds a snail shell no longer occupied, and pushes its soft abdomen into it. It then hunts for an anemone. Having found one it takes the anemone in a claw and holds it just below its mouth. The anemone attaches itself there, and grows upward in two lobes that meet and fuse over the snail shell. It also gives out a horny membrane that covers the shell, and actually enlarges it, since it extends beyond the shell's limits. As a result the crab does not have to change shells so often as it grows. However, when one shell definitely is too samll and it must move to a larger one,

Hermit crab in "borrowed" shell with symbiotic partners— anemone, barnacles, and hydroids— attached

39

it takes along its anemone partner, which goes without any struggle. If a person tries to pull an anemone from the spot to which it is anchored, it clings stubbornly!

The mutual benefit is a matter of food and protection. When the crab eats, plentiful scraps of food come within reach of *Adamsia palliata*. At all times the stinging tentacles of the anemone give protection to the crab. There are many other associations between anemones and crabs, particularly the hermit, but none so close as these two. Apparently *Adamsia palliata* cannot live without its crab host.

Not so dependent is the "shark sucker" fish, Remora, which owes its popular name to its association with sharks. Remora has a very special kind of fin by which it can firmly attach itself to a shark (although sometimes another kind of large fish is adopted as a partner). Then it may make its way into a gill cavity or the mouth as a place of refuge. Not only does it have protection and transportation in such a spot, it helps itself to some of the food of its host. However, it does the shark no harm, and it can swim strongly and rapidly on its own when not "hitchhiking."

Not all strange underwater partnerships belong to the deep seas. Some are to be found in freshwater ponds and streams. One of them is between the swan mussel and the bitterling fish. A female and male mussel each dig a hideaway, close by each other, in the bottom of a pond. Only two little tubes protrude from each body, extending just above the surface of the mud. Through them the mussels pull in water, obtaining thereby a supply of oxygen and food. Then they expel it again. Early in the summer, eggs begin to form in the lining of the female's shell; later these move out into her gills. At this point she leaves her retreat for

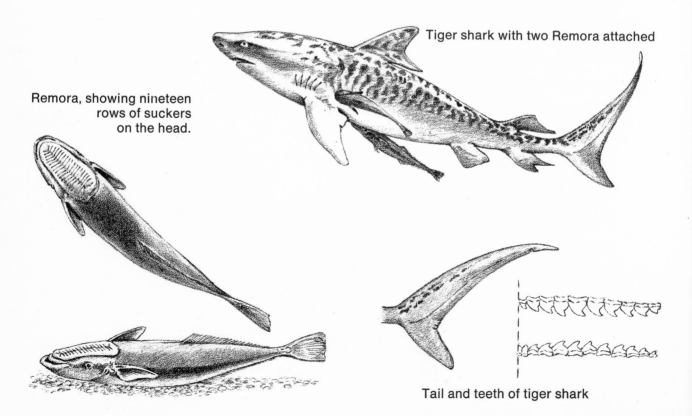

Tiger shark with two Remora attached

Remora, showing nineteen rows of suckers on the head.

40

Tail and teeth of tiger shark

the freedom of the water. The male also leaves his, and sends out a cloud of sperm. At once the female draws them in, and they pass by her gills and the eggs.

Thus fertilized, the eggs begin to develop. In a few weeks they are actually tiny mussels with shells, although their adult organs are still incomplete. They are too large to remain in the mother's gill chamber, yet they are unable to take care of themselves. How are they to survive this stage?

One day a bitterling swims close by the mussel. She also is involved in raising a family, and carries a number of eggs within her body. As she passes near, the mollusk opens her shell and her young ones pour out. Many of them immediately clamp on to the sides or the fins of the bitterling, using the two interlocking teeth that have already formed on their shells. There they stay as the bitterling's flesh swells from the irritation caused by the bites. The young mussels gradually become completely enclosed and live on the flesh which surrounds them.

About a month passes as the mussels grow at the expense of their foster-parent. Then, at last ready to begin independent lives, they break loose, leaving the bitterling wounded but healthy. In time the wounds heal, and she is none the worse for the experience.

Meanwhile the bitterling's own eggs have been taken care of—within the mussel's shell! While the young mussels were attaching themselves to her body, she was busy putting her eggs—by means of a long ovipositor—into the flesh of the mussel mother. The eggs have not yet been fertilized, but this is taken care of as a male bitterling sheds his sperm close by. Promptly it is drawn between her shells by the mussel, and it passes through the gills where the bitterling eggs are resting. Thus, as the bitterling plays foster-parent to the young mussels, the female mussel protects and nourishes the young bitterlings until they are ready for independence. It is a successful two-way helpfulness.

Mussels are often involved with other partners. There are small, round-bodied "pea crabs" that take advantage of the spaces in the mussel's mantle cavity. They enter by means of the inhaling siphon, and they may leave again just as easily as they entered. But often a little crab remains for a long time. It is safe there, and it can feed on the larger bits of food that are drawn in by the mussel.

Bitterling female laying eggs in a freshwater mussel. The male bitterling swims nearby.

41

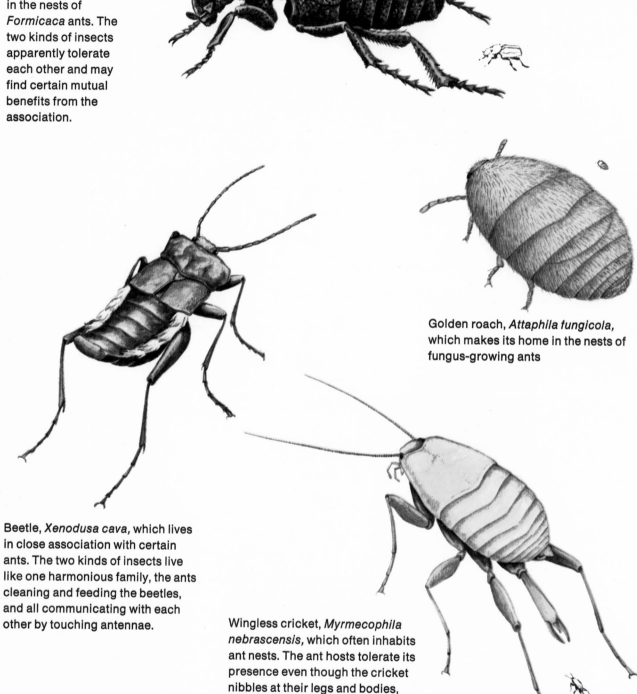

Beetle, *Cremastocheilus castanea,* which lives in the nests of *Formicaca* ants. The two kinds of insects apparently tolerate each other and may find certain mutual benefits from the association.

Golden roach, *Attaphila fungicola,* which makes its home in the nests of fungus-growing ants

Beetle, *Xenodusa cava,* which lives in close association with certain ants. The two kinds of insects live like one harmonious family, the ants cleaning and feeding the beetles, and all communicating with each other by touching antennae.

Wingless cricket, *Myrmecophila nebrascensis,* which often inhabits ant nests. The ant hosts tolerate its presence even though the cricket nibbles at their legs and bodies, from which are obtained a beneficial oily secretion.

42

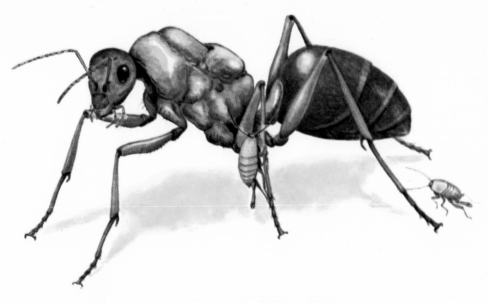

Ant with crickets nibbling at its legs

In the Insect World

It is not surprising that many kinds of ants are involved with a number of partners or permanent visitors to their colonies. Their way of life—as they build elaborate nests, store food supplies, and give painstaking care to members of the colony— offers the possibility of benefits to many small creatures. And a number of them do move into ant colonies and make themselves at home.

Among the permanent guests of some ants are certain beetles—the staphylinids. When these tiny beetles, which are somewhat antlike in appearance, move into an ant colony, their future is assured. The ants helpfully take care of their young when they are born, and seem to mind not at all when the adult beetles eat some of the young ants. The beetles also obtain nourishment by stroking the ants, causing them to disgorge food for their benefit. On the other hand, the beetles secrete a liquid substance which is eagerly licked up by the ants. Some of the staphylinid beetles even team up with colonies of army ants that have no nests, and move about with them in their wanderings.

There is a very small roach, golden in color, so closely connected with certain ants that it has been named for them. The ants are the *Attas*, a species living in Central and South America that make fungus gardens under the earth's surface, and the roach is called *Attaphila*, meaning "friend of the Atta." These roaches spend their entire existence in the nests of the fungus-growers, and because of the countless years they have spent in darkness, they have lost their sight. They constantly lick secretions from the coats of the worker ants, thus providing themselves with nourishment and helping to keep the ants clean.

A partnership between certain ants and the plant lice known as aphids may, at first, not seem a real partnership. In fact, the relationship is usually compared with dairy farmers and their cows, as the ants keep the aphids in specially constructed "sheds," and may move them about from place to place at their own convenience. However, the aphids have definite benefits from the arrangement. The ants protect them from other predatory insects and provide them with shelter. They even remove earth from plant roots and then construct passageways to them by which the aphids can easily reach this food supply.

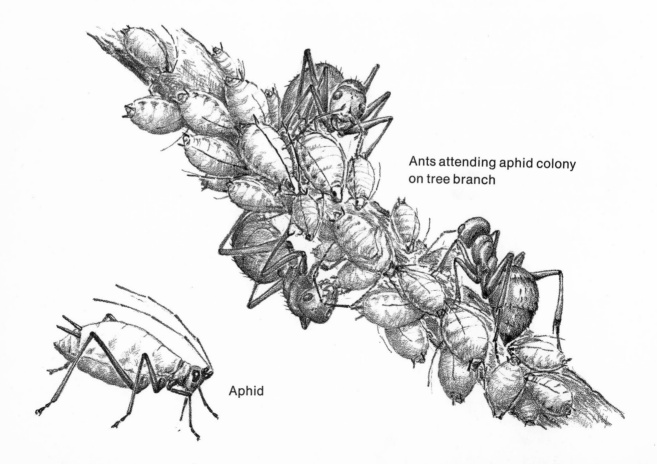

Ants attending aphid colony
on tree branch

Aphid

The aphids give something in return—a liquid, rich in sugars that is a favorite food of ants. When an ant taps an aphid on the back with its antenna, a drop of the "honeydew" is promptly given out.

Some kinds of ants and aphids are almost completely dependent on each other. One such close relationship is between the cornfield ant and corn root aphid. During the winter the ants give remarkable care to the aphid eggs, carrying them from one place to another as moisture and temperature conditions change. In the spring, when the eggs hatch, the ants carry the young to plant roots, where they can immediately start feeding. By summer, as the aphids increase to vast numbers, the ants carry many of them to more distant roots, and the population is thus distributed.

Certain beetles and several true bugs have come to resemble ants in body shape, markings, and manner of walking. They attach themselves to a colony and, if not quickly detected and put out by the ants, they become permanent partners— even acquiring the distinctive odor of that particular nest. It is the mimic that receives all the benefits, as the ants continue their industrious quest for food and bring it to the nest for the entire colony to share. The mimics even beg drops of regurgitated nourishment, and often the ants oblige.

A nearly perfect example of mutualism is found among the termites and certain protozoa. It is common knowledge that many termites eat wood; in fact this is

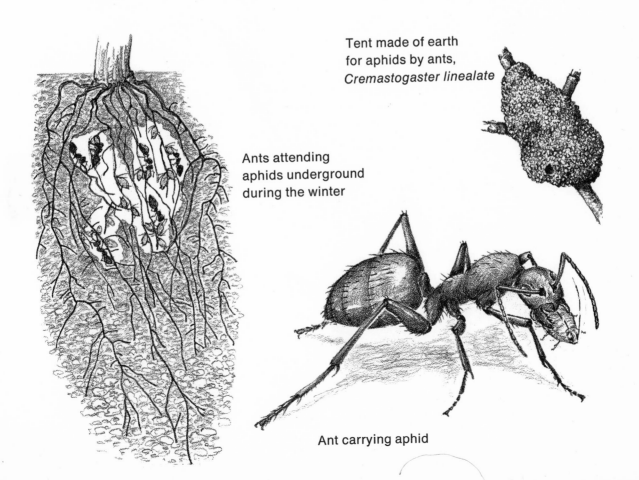

Tent made of earth for aphids by ants, *Cremastogaster linealate*

Ants attending aphids underground during the winter

Ant carrying aphid

45

the complete diet of certain species. Yet termites cannot digest cellulose, which is the major substance in wood. How, then, are they nourished?

There are minute organisms—different species of bacteria and protozoa—that live in the termite's digestive tract. They *are* able to digest cellulose. As the termites supply them with bits of wood, they flourish. In return they supply a substance which dissolves some wood for the termites; and as they die, their bodies help to nourish the termites. These partners are so dependent on each other that, when separated, neither one survives.

Every new generation of termites is able to carry along the relationship with the tiny partners because the young eat the droppings of the adults. Contained in the droppings are some protozoans which multiply rapidly and are carried to new colonies by young queens and kings. Termites that do not have protozoa partners eat fungi and bacteria.

Other insects also have symbiotic protozoa in their bodies. Among them are certain roaches which, like the termites, eat wood and depend on the portozoa to digest it. A large species, *Cryptocercus*, is one of these.

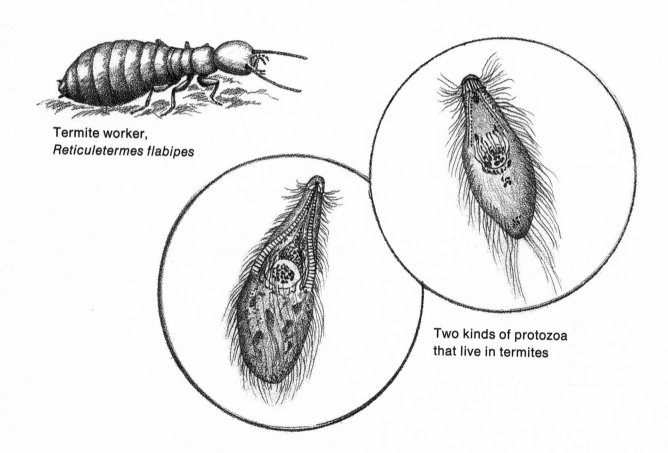

Termite worker,
Reticuletermes flabipes

Two kinds of protozoa
that live in termites

Big and Little

The very tiny creatures living within the bodies of small insects are not likely to have a direct bearing on the lives of people. But there are other similar partnerships of minute animals living inside big ones that do have influence—good or bad—on man's health and welfare.

Among those that cause serious trouble are a species of *Trypanosoma*, which is responsible for the dreaded African sleeping sickness. It is generally said that this disease is spread by the tsetse fly. But the protozoa *Trypanosoma* is the originator of the trouble. It lives in the blood of some African antelopes. If a tsetse fly sucks the blood of one of these, the protozoa may be transferred to its body and multiply rapidly in the insect's salivary juices. Then if the fly bites a person, the protozoa enters the human blood stream. Although the trypanosomes do no harm to their antelope partner, they quickly create a poison in a human that may be followed by his losing consciousness and his eventual death.

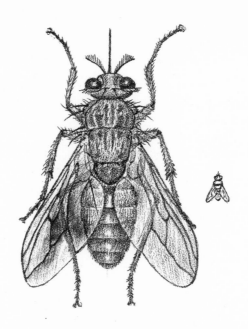

Tsetse fly of Africa, *Glossina palpalis*

Other species of the same protozoa are disastrous to horses and cattle in Africa and Asia. They all lead complicated lives in a series of "little partner" relationships, and do their damage to domestic animals when carried to them by flies.

In contrast to the trouble caused by invisible little partners of large animals, there are others which are a necessity to the existence of cattle, sheep, and goats. These and other ruminant mammals can, by themselves, digest only the smallest fraction of the dry grass they eat. When first swallowed, vegetation goes unchewed into the first part of a four-part stomach. There it mixes with a semi-liquid rich in bacteria that splits the cellulose of the grass. Later, while the animal is resting quietly, the food is transferred, a lump at a time, to a second section where it is formed into a ball. This is called the "cud"; the cud is regurgitated to the animal's mouth. There it is chewed thoroughly so that fibers are broken down and well integrated with the bacteria. Again the food is swallowed, and this time it goes on to the third and fourth stomachs.

All the big-little associations are not concerned with small internal partners; there are some quite small animals that live on the outside of larger kinds. Small moths of the family *Tineidae* often attach themselves to hairy animals for egg-laying. When the eggs hatch, the larvae uses hair or fur as food. There is reason why the manes of many lions have a "moth-eaten" look—they *have* been moth-eaten—by growing larvae. Sloths from South America are often found with large numbers of small moths in their hair. Though scientists have thoroughly searched the coats of these mammals, however, they have never discovered the insects' larvae—at least none that they recognized. But the adult moths have been seen taking moisture from the eyes and nostrils of their host.

Moths of this same family are the familiar pests known as clothes-moths. They invade people's closets and storage places, laying their eggs on fabrics of animal origin such as wool, fur, and felts. In a remote sense, they may be considered unwelcome partners of humans!

The hair of some mammals, such as a lion's mane, furnishes a good breeding place for certain insects

Some of the most dreaded little pests that attach themselves to large animals are the botflies. Though thay are somewhat larger than the common house fly, they are small indeed, compared with horses, sheep, and other mammals to which they attach themselves.

The true horse botfly fastens its eggs to the hairs or skin of its hosts with a cementlike substance that is very irritating. The horse rubs the spot on which it has been placed with his nose, and may lick it. As a result the eggs are aided in hatching and the larvae enter the horse's mouth. Various species of fly attach themselves to various parts of their host's anatomy—pharynx, stomach, or the intestine—and, feeding on blood, they remain until mature larvae. Then they pass on out of the body with waste matter, become pupae in the soil, and develop into adults which quickly attach themselves to any horse nearby.

The sheep botfly has the amazing habit of laying living larvae in the nostrils of its unfortunate partner—doing so without alighting.

Cows resting quietly,
chewing the "cud"

A more pleasant type of big-little partnership is that which exists between certain luminescent fish and bacteria. Luminosity is an advantage at many times in the darkness of the underwater world. It may help attract food toward a fish, or it may be a means of defense. Some fish—mostly those that live in the ocean—actually have the power to produce light. They may secrete luminous chemicals from pits in the skin or use organs which contain light. However, in other fish luminous bacteria may be the cause. They stow away in a number of small pockets of the skin and, especially if there is mirrorlike tissue behind them, they shine out quite strongly.

The lamp-eyed fish has an extraordinary arrangement for its bacteria partners. Just below each eye is a mass of tubes, separated by blood vessels containing millions of bacteria. The bacteria live on food and oxygen extracted from the blood, and they produce a luminous chemical. Below each shining mass is a fold of tissue. To shut off its light, the fish simply draws up the tissue, and a complete "black-out" is achieved.

Luminous fish showing, under the eye, effect of bacteria partners

Rhinoceros with tick birds

Birds and Beasts

It seems strange that a bird and the type of animal aptly described as a beast would form a partnership. Yet sometimes they do.

One of the oddest combinations is that of a bird and that giant reptile, the crocodile. Some scientists still ask for proof that there is a definite partnership between the two, but it has been reported many, many times, and it is so firmly believed in that the bird—a lapwing—is commonly called the crocodile bird.

This black and white lapwing is found in southwestern Asia, on the shores of the Mediterranean, and in much of Africa. It is especially numerous in Egypt. There it frequents the shores of fresh-water swamps and streams, encountering the crocodiles as they come out of the water to sun themselves. When a crocodile opens its mouth, a bird hops in. But it is not eaten. Instead it performs a dental service of feeding on leeches while the crocodile obligingly keeps its jaws from closing.

Similarly, sun bitterns of South America serve tapirs by removing ticks from them, at the same time providing themselves with food. In Africa there are other birds that serve rhinoceroses and camels in the same way.

New Zealand has an unusual animal partnership in a bird and a reptile called the tuatara, which is lizardlike in appearance, but distinct enough from the lizard to be classed in a family by itself. Often it is described as a living fossil because it belongs to a group of ancient reptiles that date back to the early days of the dinosaurs. During the period of time in which dinosaurs were developing into gigantic forms, this group was gradually dying away until at last only the tuatara survived.

Today tuataras live only on some of the smaller islands of New Zealand, which are home also to colonies of petrels or "mutton birds." These birds and reptiles share underground burrows. The birds make them in the deep layer of humus that lies under the branches of a low tree, *Coprosma*. So numerous are the burrows that the whole humus layer is riddled with them, but a never-ceasing wind sweeps falling leaves and twigs into each burrow opening. The birds constantly work over them and, in doing so, mix them with feathers, bits of eggshells, and other debris. The result is an upper layer of soil, in some places two feet deep, that is uniform in color and composition.

The tuataras can, and do, to some extent, burrow for themselves. But mostly they make use of the petrels' nests, and the partners seem to get along in friendly enough fashion. The reptile lays its eggs in a shallow excavation usually a distance

Tapir and South American bird

away from the home shared with the bird. Eggs are laid in September or October and require about a year to hatch. The adult tuataras are about two feet in length, although some grow to be larger.

The petrel's egg (only one is laid at a time) is incubated in the burrow for an eight-week period. The baby bird remains there for about seven weeks during which its parents provide its food.

A mistaken belief is held by many people that a similar partnership between a bird and a reptile and a mammal exists in the United States, the animals involved being burrowing owls, rattlesnakes, and gophers. The three are said often to share a home on the open prairies and grasslands where they all live. However, in this case, there is no "living together." Burrowing owls and rattlesnakes do show up in gopher burrows, but they are looking for prey. A young prairie dog makes a fine meal for either. Or the owls may take over burrows dug by prairie dogs, then deserted, and use them for nesting.

New Zealand Tuatara

Mutton bird in burrow

On the African plains there is an association between birds and mammals that affords mutual help, although the two do not establish a home together. The bird in this case is the large, flightless ostrich.

Ostriches frequently roam about the great open regions in a constant search for food with such four-footed animals as zebra and wildebeest. The birds, having a seven-foot neck stretch, can see far into the distant landscape. If they notice anything that suggests danger, they start running in the opposite direction, and the mammals go along with them. On the other hand, the mammals flush quantities of "game," such as small reptiles, mammals, and insects from the underbrush, and the ostriches feed on them, though they also enjoy fruits, seeds, and plants.

Wildebeest, zebra, and ostrich—frequent companions on the plains of Africa

Another bird of Africa, a great contrast to the ostrich in appearance and habits, has a most unusual type of partnership with mammals. The bird is the honey guide, a relative of woodpeckers, and about the size of a starling. Its frequent partner is the honey badger, or ratal, a furry creature no larger than a wildcat. Or it may have as a teammate a person native to the African forests. What brings bird and beast or man together, is a mutual interest in honeybees.

The honey guide's concern with a beehive is the bees themselves as well as the honey. These birds are insect eaters, and they also have a great craving for beeswax. Wild bees' nests may be plentiful, and the honey guide may locate one quite easily, but then it is frustrated. It has only a small bill, and no means of breaking into the hive!

Now the search for a partner begins. The bird starts a rasping chatter and flies about until it attracts the attention of a honey badger—or a person. Having succeeded in this, it may return to the nest already discovered or it locates another, while its partner follows along. Then it stops its chattering and flies around in little circles or settles on a high limb of a tree. Soon its partner will see a stream of bees going in and out of a small opening in a hollow in the tree (or it may be in a large termite nest), and knows the honey feast is at hand.

When the partner is a honey badger, this eager hunter quickly goes into action. Working with powerful legs and strong claws, he quickly tears open the nesting site and helps himself to honey and bee grubs. The bees' attempts to drive him away are not successful because of his very thick hair. The bird waits and watches. When the badger has had his fill, he moves away. Then the honey guide moves in. There is always some honey left, and some bee grubs. And there is sure to be some wax—a substance that the honey guide alone, of all animals, can digest and use as a source of nourishment.

Today there are not so many human partners interested in teaming up with honey guides; more often the natives construct hives to attract wild bees near their homes. But there is still some of this ancient kind of honey-hunting. Working with a bird, a man usually locates a hive in about half an hour. He breaks into it or cuts it open with a knife, working with one hand and shielding himself from the angry bees with the other, in which he holds a smoking faggot. He helps himself liberally to honey, but always leaves a share for his feathered partner.

The honey guide has still another unusual habit. Instead of building a nest in which to lay its eggs, the female manages to sneak into the nest of some other bird and lay her single egg there. Honey guides are not alone in this strange behavior; several other kinds of birds do the same thing, among them some American cowbirds.

57

Ratel and Honey guide

There are various species of cowbirds in the New World. The one that lives in the eastern United States is very common. In size and coloring it is quite similar to blackbirds, but its habit of entrusting the fate of its baby to other birds is very different from the behavior of any other American bird.

Male and female cowbird never "pair off" to establish a home and family. They move about in flocks, often bobbing around in the field close behind cattle so they can grab any insects stirred up by the big animals' feet. This is one partnership in which they are involved, and it works no hardship on their chosen allies. It is a different story, however, when they make unsuspecting partners of other birds. The partner's family may suffer disaster as a result.

When the female cowbird is ready to deposit her single egg, she looks about for the nest of some smaller bird. When she finds one that is unguarded—and preferably with eggs already in it—she quickly drops her own egg there, then flies away. The owner of the nest possibly a song sparrow—returning, pays no attention to the fact that a strange egg, one larger than her own, has been added. She settles down to brood again.

Presently the eggs hatch, and one baby is bigger and stronger than the rest. But again the little mother sparrow may take no notice. She begins her endless job of food-finding and feeding. And because the young cowbird has a longer neck and bigger mouth than the other babies, it gets the greater share. Sometimes the rightful babies of a nest become so undernourished they die. Or, as they grow weaker, the rapidly growing cowbird may push them out of the nest. Still the mother sparrow is unaware of the deception. She gives all her energy to the care and feeding of her "foster child."

Some birds, such as yellow warblers, are alert enough to avoid such a destructive partnership. When a strange egg is left with them, they notice. And they build a new nest on top of the first one so that the egg—along with their own eggs—are left unhatched underneath. If the cowbird returns and deposits another egg in the second nest, they build a third nest on top of the second.

Warbler nests have been found in a series of three—one on top of another. Evidence of what had happened in this drama of the bird world was given by unhatched eggs. In the bottom nest was an unhatched cowbird egg; in the second, an unhatched cowbird egg and warbler egg. The third nest sheltered a full quota of warbler eggs, and in it was no cowbird intruder. The warbler obviously had won its battle to prevent having an unwanted partner!

Beyond Symbiosis

When we think about a plant or animal being very closely involved with some other plant or animal, it may seem that this association is the whole of existence to the two partners. But partners, as well as individual forms of life, are involved also with other living things. In any natural community the plants and animals are dependent on each other in various ways, together forming a vast web of life.

It is important that people understand this "web," for if any part of it is badly damaged or destroyed, the entire structure may perish. Plants or animals that are destroyed because they are considered undesirable often are essential to forms of life that are much needed.

A branch of science is concerned with the web of nature. This branch is called "ecology," based on the Greek words for "a study of the home." But it has a far broader meaning than that which we usually give to "home." Ecology concerns knowledge that has to do with relationships between all living organisms and their environments.

Some happenings concerned with the damaging of the web of nature are all too easy to observe. You may see grasses, trees and other vegetation cleared from a large area and, before long, find that dust storms or floods are resulting, destroying animals of every kind.

Then there are less spectacular series of events not so easily followed. For example, in a certain area efforts were being made to increase the fish population in lakes and streams. Fishing was prohibited, but still no increase in the number of fish came about. Presently it was discovered that over-grazing by cattle along the banks of the waterways had drastically reduced plant life—the kind in which countless insects could flourish. Many insects falling from the plants into the stream had once supplied food for fish. Without this abundance, the fish simply did not thrive.

The loss of plants bringing about a disappearance of insects which, in turn, kept fish from increasing in numbers, is one small episode. But in every natural community—forest, desert, meadow, ocean, lake, or pond—some of its members are the food supply of others. On land it is the green plants that provide a great amount of nourishment. Then, many of the animals such as rabbits, deer, and countless insects, that eat the vegetation, are the food of flesh-eating animals. The effect of bacteria on dead plants and animals is to turn them into fertilizer that benefits growing plants.

Even before people began to form communities of their own, human activities have influenced the natural communities. In modern times, with the building of huge cities, the spread of ranches, the cultivation of enormous farmlands, many forms of life have suffered. Some have been completely destroyed. Now efforts are being made to correct the destruction that occurs when the balance of nature is upset. And ecology is taking its place as one of the most important of all studies. People learn from it how to become partners of wildlife rather than its destroyers.

THE WEB OF LIFE

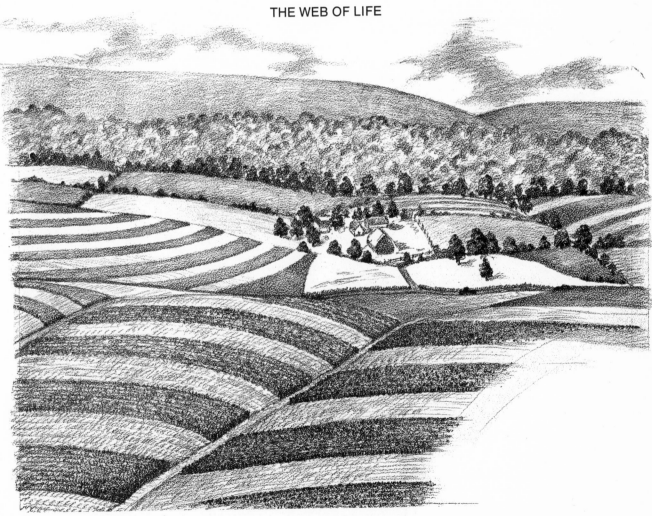

In nature's intricate web, woodlands may border on meadows and the meadows on waterways; sun-drenched hills may slope into wet valleys. In any natural community an endless variety of plants and animals may thrive. Changes take place, but slowly. It is the drastic actions of man that can quickly upset the balance of nature and cause a countryside to be despoiled.

Index

62

Nature Books for Young People

by Dorothy Shuttlesworth:
ANIMAL CAMOUFLAGE
THE AGE OF REPTILES
THE DOUBLEDAY FIRST GUIDE TO ROCKS
THE REAL BOOK ABOUT PREHISTORIC LIFE
A SENSE OF WONDER
THE STORY OF CATS
THE STORY OF DOGS
THE STORY OF HORSES

by Su Zan Noquchi Swain:
THE DOUBLEDAY FIRST GUIDE TO INSECTS
INSECTS IN THEIR WORLD
PLANTS OF WOODLAND AND WAYSIDE

by Dorothy Shuttlesworth, illustrated by Su Zan N. Swain:
NATURAL PARTNERSHIPS
THE STORY OF ANTS
THE STORY OF SPIDERS
THE STORY OF ROCKS

About the Author

Dorothy Shuttlesworth has been exploring nature since she started working for The American Museum of Natural History in New York at the age of seventeen. After several years there on the staff of *Natural History* magazine, she became the first editor of a similar magazine for young people—*Junior Natural History*—a position she held for twelve years.

Although in recent years she has been occupied more as a homemaker than as a writer, she has authored more than a dozen books on nature and science as well as many magazine articles.

In addition to this full schedule, she finds time for Women's Club work, particularly in conservation, and is active in other community projects. Mrs. Shuttlesworth is also a member of the executive board of New Jersey Citizens for Clean Air, Inc. She lives in East Orange, New Jersey, with her husband, who is a high school principal. Her son has recently married and her daughter is a student at the University of Kentucky.

About the Artist

Su Zan Noguchi Swain holds a Bachelor of Fine Arts degree from the University of Colorado but has studied basic courses in various fields of natural science and has been illustrating nature subjects since 1938.

She makes a great effort to get out in the fields to observe and to collect live models and to sketch and to photograph. With her husband and sons she has studied nature in all parts of the United States end while living in Nicaragua collected in other Central and South American countries. Travelling abroad is one of her hobbies and she has recently gathered material from Europe, the Middle East, Southeastern Asia, the Far East, and the South Pacific. When live specimens are not available or practical, she obtains preserved specimens from natural science museums and from private collections. She works under close supervision of experts since accuracy is her foremost objective.